It's My
STATE!

VIRGINIA

The Old Dominion State

Anna Maria Johnson,
Laura L. Sullivan, David C. King II,
and Stephanie Fitzgerald

Cavendish
Square

New York

VIRGINIA

The Old
Dominion
State

Statehood

June 25, 1788

Population

8,470,020
(2017 census estimate)

Capital

Richmond

State Flag and State Seal

Virginia's flag shows the state seal on a blue background. The seal shows a picture of a woman, the Roman goddess of virtue, dressed in a warrior's tunic. She stands with her left foot on the chest of a defeated warrior that represents tyranny. She holds a spear in her right hand and a sword in her left. At the bottom of the seal is a Latin phrase that means "Thus Always to Tyrants," *sic semper tyrannis*.

HISTORICAL EVENTS TIMELINE

~15,000 BCE

Humans start to inhabit the region later called Virginia.

1584

Sir Walter Raleigh names a large region of North America "Virginia." The area includes modern Virginia, as well as other states.

1607

English colonists begin to settle Jamestown.

State Song

Virginia's original state song was retired in 1997. For eighteen years, the state lacked a state song. Then, in 2015, Governor Terry McAuliffe signed into law two state songs: one traditional and one popular. "Our Great Virginia," with lyrics by Mike Greenly, is the traditional song. "Sweet Virginia Breeze," by Richmond-based musicians Robbin Thompson and Steve Bassett, is the popular song.

State Tree and State Flower

The American dogwood is both Virginia's state tree and its state flower. There are seventeen species of dogwood native to North America. They have pink or white blossoms with four petals.

1624
King Charles I of English proclaims Virginia the first royal colony.

1789
Virginian George Washington becomes the first president of the United States. (Four of the first five presidents were from Virginia.)

1831
Nat Turner, a Virginia slave, leads a rebellion that lasts two days. About sixty white people are killed, and Turner is hanged.

State Insect

Tiger Swallowtail Butterfly

State Shell

Virginia Oyster

State Bird

Northern Cardinal

1959

Thanks to the work of activists, politicians, and lawyers like Oliver Hill, Virginia public schools begin the process of desegregation.

1962

Washington Dulles International Airport opens.

1990

Douglas Wilder becomes governor of Virginia. He is the first African American to be voted governor in the nation.

State Dog

American Foxhound

State Salamander

Red Salamander

CURRENT EVENTS TIMELINE

2007
Queen Elizabeth II of England visits Jamestown to honor the four hundredth anniversary of the English settlement.

2011
Virginia experiences a rare earthquake.

2017
The Katherine G. Johnson Computational Research Facility opens in Langley. Johnson was a "human computer" who calculated trajectories for early space flights.

Skyline Drive in
Shenandoah National Park
winds its way through the
Blue Ridge Mountains.

1 Geography

Virginia is a large state rich in plants, animals, rock formations, and bodies of water. Virginia's five geographic regions include the Coastal Plain/Tidewater, the Piedmont, the Blue Ridge Mountains, the Valley and Ridge, and the Appalachian Plateau. Each region is home to its own mixture of plants and animals. Because Virginia borders the Atlantic coast, it was among the earliest parts of North America to be explored by Europeans and colonized.

Virginia has 39,490 square miles (102,279 square kilometers) of land area. It is the thirty-sixth largest state. It is made up of ninety-five counties, plus thirty-eight independent cities. Richmond is the state capital, but Virginia Beach is the city with the biggest population.

The state includes a remarkable variety of landforms for its size. The coastal region includes marshy lowlands, beautiful sand beaches, and a large swamp area. Moving inland, the lowlands change into the rolling hills of the Piedmont. Still farther west lie two mountain ranges with dramatic views and hundreds of miles of hiking trails. Nestled between the Blue Ridge Mountains and the Allegheny Mountains is the scenic and **fertile** Shenandoah Valley, treasured for its agriculture, scenery, history, and caverns.

The Chesapeake Bay

The geography of eastern Virginia is dominated by Chesapeake Bay—a huge arm of the Atlantic Ocean. The bay reaches more than 200 miles (320 kilometers) inland. The long, narrow strip of land that forms the eastern boundary of the bay is called the Delmarva Peninsula. The word "Delmarva" was created out of the names of the three states that occupy the strip of land: Delaware, Maryland, and Virginia. Some Virginians call the region the Eastern Shore. Until a series of bridges and tunnels were completed connecting the Eastern Shore to the mainland in 1964, residents there and on the nearby islands were quite isolated.

Offshore, or barrier, islands give this sliver of land some protection from Atlantic storms. They include Assateague and Chincoteague Islands, which are famous for their semiwild Chincoteague ponies.

Chesapeake Bay is a unique body of water. It is America's largest **estuary**. More than 150 of Virginia's major rivers and streams empty into the Chesapeake, including the Potomac, Rappahannock, York, and James Rivers. A broad inlet connects Chesapeake Bay with the James River to form Hampton Roads, one of the world's largest natural harbors. In 1862, during the Civil War, Hampton Roads was the scene of the world's first clash between two ironclad warships. The USS *Monitor* faced off against the CSS *Virginia* (often called the *Merrimack*—its name while part of the US fleet) in an effort to protect the USS *Minnesota*. Neither side won the battle, but the *Minnesota* remained unharmed. Both the *Monitor* and the *Virginia* survived the battle without much damage—and ushered in a new era of shipbuilding.

A view of the Chesapeake Bay and the Coleman Bridge in Yorktown

The warm, shallow waters of the bay are filled with schools of fish and large colonies of shellfish—oysters, clams, and the famous Chesapeake blue crabs. On most days of the year, this inland sea swarms with sailboats, speedboats, and fishing vessels.

The seaport city of Norfolk is home to nearly 250,000 people.

The Tidewater Region

Virginia's section of the Atlantic Coast region, a belt of lowland called the Coastal Plain that stretches from New York to Florida, is known as the Tidewater because ocean tides reach all the way into Chesapeake Bay and Virginia's four main rivers. From north to south, Virginia's coast measures about 112 miles (180 km), but all the inlets and bays, plus the Eastern Shore, create a coastline of more than 3,000 miles (almost 5,000 km).

The state's largest urban area is on the southern part of the Tidewater, including the port cities of Newport News and Norfolk, as well as Virginia Beach. Virginia Beach has about 35 miles (56 km) of beautiful white-sand beach lined with modern high-rise apartment buildings. Huge ports are located in Newport News and Norfolk, which is also home to the world's largest naval station.

The Great Dismal Swamp

South of the James River is an enormous wetland named the Great Dismal Swamp. This protected area is nearly 750 square miles (1,940 sq km) and extends into North Carolina.

In 1763, George Washington surveyed the swamp and saw its potential for timber production. He formed a company called the Dismal Swamp Land Company to drain and log parts of the swamp. Logging proved very successful, but along with commercial

FAST FACT

The word "watershed" refers to all the streams, rivers, and creeks that flow down in an area. Four major Virginia rivers feed into the Chesapeake Bay. Today these rivers are known as the James, York, Rappahannock, and Potomac. All the smaller rivers, streams, creeks, and even sewers that feed them are part of the Chesapeake Bay Watershed.

and residential development, it destroyed much of the ecosystem. The remaining area, which became the Great Dismal Swamp National Wildlife Refuge in 1974, is less than half the size of the original swamp.

Much of the swamp has been drained. In December 2013, a project was completed to return water to 9,580 acres (3,877 hectares) of state and federal land that were drained more than sixty years earlier.

From the mid-1600s through the 1800s, sprawling farms called **plantations** were built on the banks of the Tidewater rivers. Tobacco was the major cash crop of the early plantations, and after 1800, wheat became important.

These plantations, some of which still exist, were like independent villages. Each had its own orchard, vegetable garden, blacksmith shop, and carpenter—as well as a church. Rivers such as the James, York, and Rappahannock served as highways. Sailing ships carried the planters' crops to market towns and brought back merchandise from other East Coast cities and from Europe. Boats navigated the rivers to the Fall Line— the point where the soft Coastal Plain meets the harder rock of the inland hill country.

The Piedmont Region

West of the Tidewater is a region called the Piedmont, which means "foot of the mountain." It covers the central third of the state. The Piedmont features a rolling landscape that is about 50 miles (80 km) wide in the north, broadening to about 100 miles (160 km) wide in the south. The Piedmont stretches from the Blue Ridge Mountains in the west to the Fall Line.

As the Tidewater region filled with settlers in the early 1700s, pioneer families moved into the Piedmont. Most started small farms, but

The Blue Ridge Mountains are part of the Appalachian mountain range.

there were also a number of tobacco plantations. Family-owned farms, including apple and peach orchards, still cover the foothills of the Blue Ridge Mountains today. Some of the Piedmont is also now known as "horse country," famous for its traditions of fox hunting and horse breeding.

The Blue Ridge and Allegheny Mountains

The Blue Ridge Mountains extend from Carlisle, Pennsylvania, south into Georgia. The mountains form one of America's outstanding scenic areas. Two of the nation's most beautiful roads—Skyline Drive and the Blue Ridge Parkway—wind along the crest of these mountains and along upland meadows. The northern road, Skyline Drive, twists and turns for 105 miles (169 km), with a maximum speed limit of 35 miles per hour (56 kilometers per hour). The southern road, the Blue Ridge Parkway, extends another 469 miles (755 km), from Shenandoah National Park in northern Virginia to Great Smoky Mountains National Park in North Carolina.

In general, the Blue Ridge Mountains vary in height from 2,000 to 4,000 feet (600 to 1,200 meters). One exceptionally high point in the range—and the highest point in the state of Virginia—is Mount Rogers, which is 5,729 feet (1,746 m) above sea level.

The Blue Ridge Mountains and the more rugged Allegheny Mountains to the west are among the oldest mountains in the world. Over thousands of years, the forces of wind and water slowly wore away the jagged peaks to create more gentle landforms. The two scenic roads through the Blue Ridge provide breathtaking views of the Piedmont hills to the east and the Alleghenies to the west. The

Pink and white mountain laurels bloom each spring in Shenandoah National Park.

Virginia's Biggest Cities

(Population numbers are from the US Census Bureau's 2017 projections for incorporated cities.)

Virginia Beach

Newport News

1. Virginia Beach: population 450,435

This tourist haven on the Atlantic Ocean at the mouth of Chesapeake Bay is the largest city in Virginia and the forty-fourth largest in the United States. It has miles of beaches, as well as hundreds of restaurants and hotels.

2. Norfolk: population 244,703

The second-largest city in Virginia is part of the Hampton Roads metropolitan area, located on the mouth of the Hampton Roads natural harbor at the mouth of Chesapeake Bay. It is home to the world's largest naval base, Naval Station Norfolk.

3. Chesapeake: population 240, 397

Also in the Hampton Roads metropolitan area, Chesapeake is a diverse city where dense urban areas lie beside wilderness such as the Great Dismal Swamp. It was named the twenty-first-best city in America by *Bloomberg BusinessWeek*.

4. Richmond: population 227,032

Virginia's capital, Richmond is located along the James River. The site was an important village during the Powhatan Confederacy in the 1500s and has remained vital ever since. It served as the capital of the Confederacy during the Civil War.

5. Newport News: population 179,388

Newport News is another city in the Hampton Roads metropolitan area. Though there are several theories, the exact origin of its name is a mystery. Some believe it was named for Christopher Newport, captain of the *Susan Constant*.

6. Alexandria: population 160,035

Alexandria is in northern Virginia, close to the nation's capital, Washington, DC, and many who live there have government or military jobs. Its historic Old Town district sits on the Potomac waterfront and is home to many fine restaurants and boutiques.

Alexandria

7. Hampton: population 134,669

Located on the southeastern end of the Virginia Peninsula, Hampton is one of the seven major cities that make up the Hampton Roads metropolitan area. It is home to Langley Air Force Base and the Peninsula Town Center.

8. Roanoke: population 99,837

Roanoke is located in southwest Virginia in the Roanoke Valley. It was formerly called Big Lick, after the natural salt outcropping that formed a salt lick for such local wildlife as deer and (formerly) bison.

9. Portsmouth: population 94,572

Located on the Elizabeth River and part of the Hampton Roads metropolitan area, Portsmouth is home to the Norfolk Naval Shipyard. It has miles of waterfront and a ferry that transports people between Portsmouth and Norfolk.

Portsmouth

10. Suffolk: population 90,237

This city on the Nansemond River is another member of the Hampton Roads metropolitan area. It is known for its peanut production. It is home to Planter's Peanuts and is the birthplace of Mr. Peanut.

leaves of the hardwood trees on the slopes of the Blue Ridge—maple, hickory, white oak, and others—turn dazzling colors in the autumn.

The Allegheny Mountains, one of the ranges in the Appalachian chain, are on Virginia's border with Kentucky. For America's pioneers, these mountains formed a more imposing barrier than the Blue Ridge. It was not until 1775 that Daniel Boone led a group of woodsmen to **blaze** the Wilderness Road trail through a pass called the Cumberland Gap from southwest Virginia into what became Kentucky. Thousands of families followed Boone's road.

Oh, Shenandoah

When the first pioneers entered the Shenandoah Valley around 1700, they saw herds of bison roaming fertile grasslands watered by the Shenandoah River. By the late 1700s, the bison—and most Native American groups—had retreated farther west or died. Land-hungry settlers poured into the valley and established small family-owned farms, many of which are still in operation today.

The northern end of the valley, which is approximately 150 miles (240 km) long, is anchored by Winchester, the capital of Virginia's well-known apple orchard region. The orchards and wheat fields of the Shenandoah were important to the South during the Civil War. The valley also formed a natural north-south highway for the South's armies.

In June 1863, for example, the famous Confederate general Robert E. Lee led his Army of Northern Virginia north through the valley, using the Blue Ridge Mountains to shield his movements from the North's armies in the east. The next month, after the Confederate defeat at Gettysburg, Pennsylvania, Lee used the valley for his retreat.

Today, the Shenandoah Valley is a popular tourist area. The valley is dotted with Civil War battle sites and historic homes, including the birthplace of President Woodrow Wilson and the headquarters of Civil War general Thomas "Stonewall" Jackson. Visitors are also drawn to such natural wonders as Natural Bridge, formed by limestone, and the Luray Caverns, filled with **stalactites** and stalagmites formed over millions of years.

Mild Mid-Atlantic Seasons

The Virginia climate offers something for everyone. Along the coast, people enjoy long summers and mild winters. Farmers like the Tidewater growing season, which lasts up to eight months—three months longer than in the western part of the state. Although the Tidewater receives only a few inches of snow every year, the mountains see up to 23 inches (58 cm).

The overall climate of Virginia is mild. But the ocean affects weather and climate, making summers generally cooler near the coast, and winters less severe. January temperatures close to sea level average about 42 degrees Fahrenheit (6 degrees Celsius), while in the mountains, the average January temperature is about 31°F (−1°C).

Visitors to Luray Caverns can see how stalactites and stalagmites form.

Diverse Wildlife

Forests cover about 62 percent of Virginia's land area. Some of the state's most common trees include oaks, pines, maples, hickories, and beeches. In the fall, many of the leaves turn brilliant shades of orange, red, or yellow. The state has many different types of plants, including ferns and native grasses. In warmer months, redbuds, lilies, azaleas, mountain laurels, and bluebells color the woodland paths and roadsides.

Early Maps and Borders of Virginia

Virginia was named in honor of England's Queen Elizabeth I, whose nickname was the "Virgin Queen" because she never married. In 1588, Thomas Hariot published *A Briefe and True Report of the New Found Land of Virginia*. The large area he called "Virginia" included not just the present-day state but also part of today's North Carolina, Maryland, and more. Artist John White made paintings and sketches of the same region, including images of the Native people, whom the English called "Indians." His drawings were the earliest European pictures of Native Americans. In 1590, John White's map of "Virginia" was published along with Hariot's book. White's map was the first to identify the Chesapeake Bay by name: "Chesepiooc Sinus." Both Hariot and White had been part of an expedition to explore and settle North America's eastern coast sponsored by Sir Walter Raleigh.

In 1606, King James I granted a land charter to the Virginia Company. That charter gave the company a sweeping territory north to south, from New York to South Carolina. Virginia's second charter, in 1609, extended its western border to the Pacific Ocean, which is as far as today's California! At that time, the English had no idea how large the continent really was.

Another key map of Virginia was published by John Smith, who was important in settling Jamestown, in 1612. It was so detailed that explorers trusted it for almost seventy years. It even included the locations of important Native America settlements. Between 1612 and 1624, many versions of Smith's Virginia map were printed. John Smith described his first impressions of the Powhatan River (today known as the James River). In his book *A True Relation of Such Occurrences and Accidents of Note, as Hath Hapned in Virginia,* he told of "great craggy

John Smith's famous map of Virginia features a drawing of Chief Powhatan.

stones … in the midst of the river, where the water falleth so rudely, and with such a violence" that no boat could pass. Next to this river, "the south side is plaine low ground, and the north side high mountains, the rockes being of a gravelly nature, interlaced with many vains of glistring spangles."

In 1753, surveyors Joshua Fry and Peter Jefferson published a more accurate map of Virginia that is now treasured by museums and collectors. It marked the borders between Virginia and Maryland, Pennsylvania, North Carolina, and New Jersey. It also showed the entire Virginia river system for the first time. Interestingly, Peter Jefferson was the father of Thomas Jefferson, who later became the third president of the United States.

Geese migrate along the Eastern Shore of Virginia.

Thanks to its varied landscapes and ecosystems, Virginia is home to an incredible array of wildlife. Mammals such as deer and raccoons can be found in most areas. The state's fourteen wildlife refuges include all types of habitats, from forests to marshes. Black bears, river otters, bobcats, and many bird species live in remote places such as the Great Dismal Swamp. Virginia Beach is a great location to see pods of dolphins frolicking in the surf. Chesapeake Bay is on the Atlantic Flyway, the path that many birds take when traveling south to warmer temperatures for the winter and then traveling north again in spring. In spring and autumn, thousands of migrating birds pause to rest on the area's many islands and on the Eastern Shore. More than two hundred species have been identified, including many kinds of shorebirds. Geese, ducks, herons, and other water birds make their homes in or near Virginia waterways.

The state's bodies of water are home to fish and amphibians. Trout, pike, perch, sunfish, bass, and catfish live in the lakes, rivers, ponds, and streams. Striped bass, American shad, and herring swim through the waters of Chesapeake Bay. Moist land in swamps and near lakes, rivers, and streams is ideal for amphibians such as frogs, toads, and salamanders.

A Home for Everyone

Virginia is home to both very common and very rare plant and animal species. For example, the nation's first endangered bee, the rusty-patched bumblebee, has been found in the state. Meanwhile, bright orange Eastern newts are easy to find in moist, wooded areas. Virginians enjoy their varied environments both for making a living and for recreation.

Chincoteague National Wildlife Refuge and Assateague Island

Along Virginia's Eastern Shore lie barrier islands that are separated from the mainland. This separation has created the chance for animals on the islands to develop differently than those on the mainland. Island animals tend to become smaller over many, many years. Semiwild horses have lived on Assateague Island for more than three hundred years. They've grown small but strong as they have had to survive extreme heat, insects, storms, and poor-quality food.

Even though they are genetically horses, they look like ponies because they are small and have rounded bellies.

This is because they have adapted to eat saltmarsh cordgrass, saltmeadow hay, and beach grass. Because these grasses are salty, the horses drink twice as much water as domesticated horses.

Chincoteague's horses draw visitors from all over.

There is a Virginia herd and a Maryland herd of these horses. The herds are kept separate by a fence that runs across the Maryland/Virginia state line on the island. The two herds are managed differently.

Each year, on the last Wednesday of July, the Virginia horses are rounded up, and they swim to nearby Chincoteague Island. Visitors come from all over to watch. This event inspired a famous book in 1947. Marguerite Henry's *Misty of Chincoteague* describes a special horse named Misty. The characters in the novel were real, though events were changed for the story.

What Lives in Virginia?

Eastern brook trout

Tiger swallowtail butterfly

Virginia big-eared bat

Eastern Brook Trout Also called brookies, mountain trout, or speckled trout, these colorful fish are not as common as they were in the past. High school students in Virginia, along with the organization Trout Unlimited, have been working to raise brook trout and release them back into cold, clean creeks where they used to be abundant.

Eastern Tiger Swallowtail Butterfly The Virginia state insect is a beautiful butterfly that comes in two colors. The males are yellow with black markings like tiger stripes. The females can be yellow or black with iridescent blue lower wings and spots of orange and yellow.

Northern Red Salamander This special salamander species was chosen as a Virginia state symbol in 2018 and has been found in eighty-one Virginia counties. It is bright red-orange in color with dark spots that look like freckles. It lives in and near cold springs and streams. It breathes through its skin because it does not have lungs.

Oyster Virginians chose the oyster as their state shell in 1974. Today's many types of living oysters make Virginia famous. The Virginia Oyster Trail encourages people to visit different regions and learn about the value of oysters.

Virginia Big-Eared Bat Only three states have a state bat, including Texas and Oklahoma. Virginia chose this symbol in 2005 in order to help people learn about the importance of caves and the animals that live in them. This cute bat species with large ears is listed as endangered on the state and federal level.

What Grows in Virginia?

Coral Honeysuckle This native honeysuckle has bright pink flowers that attract butterflies and hummingbirds. It's found primarily in the Coastal Plain and Piedmont, and less commonly in the mountains. This vine also makes an excellent garden plant when grown on a trellis or other support.

Eastern Prickly Pear Cactus The Eastern prickly pear cactus is Virginia's only native cactus. It grows low to the ground, up to 6 inches (15 centimeters) tall, and appears flat with bristles or spines on it. Yellow flowers appear in June and July. The bright red fruit is edible. It attracts butterflies, bees, and birds. It can be grown in rock gardens.

Flame Azalea This shrub is related to rhododendrons. It takes its name from its bright orange flowers, which look like fire. It can grow up to 10 feet (3 m) high and 15 feet (4.5 m) wide in the Appalachian Mountains. It is one of the ten kinds of azaleas and rhododendrons native to Virginia.

Virginia Bluebells These beautiful April flowers are also called Virginia cowslip and Roanoke bells. The buds are pink, and the bell-shaped blossoms range in color from pink to various shades of blue. Thomas Jefferson grew these flowers at Monticello. In the wild, bluebells grow along wet areas.

White Oak These trees can live for hundreds of years. The white oak is a dominant tree in eastern North American forests. Many animals and insects use it for food and for a habitat. Unlike other types of oak, the wood is water-resistant, which is why people have used it for shipbuilding and for making wine barrels.

Coral honeysuckle

Flame azalea

Virginia bluebells

White oak

National Park Service artist Sydney King painted this picture of how the Jamestown colony might have looked around 1615.

2 The History of Virginia

As the nation's first colony, Virginia has a rich and fascinating recorded history. Documents tell the story of people settling in a new place in order to find new opportunities and to make a living. Virginia's history is also the story of people moving from bondage as **indentured servants** or slaves to freedom. Early Virginians wrote about the importance of many kinds of freedom: to think, speak, and worship freely, to own land, and to choose leaders.

The First Virginians

Scientists have established that humans moved into the area now known as Virginia at least sixteen thousand years ago. By about 1400 CE, the descendants of those early people were part of the Woodland American Indian culture that existed throughout the East. The Native Americans who first met Europeans on Virginia's Atlantic coast belonged to groups that spoke Algonquian languages.

In the late 1500s, English explorer Sir Walter Raleigh hoped to start a colony in North America. Unlike the pilgrims who traveled to Massachusetts a few decades later, the people

> **FAST FACT**
> The first free public school was set up in Hampton, Virginia, in 1634. In 1693, the College of William and Mary was founded as a "place of universal study." It was the second college in the United States, after Harvard.

Sir Walter Raleigh suggested the name "Virginia" for a large section of North America, including the site of his failed Roanoke colony.

bound for Virginia were not looking for religious freedom. They wanted economic opportunity.

Raleigh's first attempt at colonization occurred in 1585 on the island of Roanoke, in present-day North Carolina. Life was hard for the settlers, who nearly starved to death. They abandoned the region in 1586, but Raleigh tried again in 1587. Governor John White led the second group to land on Roanoke. He soon went back to England for supplies. When White returned in 1590, he found the settlement empty and no trace of his people. No one knows for sure what happened to the settlers.

In 1606, a group called the Virginia Company received a charter, or contract, from King James I of England to establish a colony in Virginia. In May 1607, three ships—the *Susan Constant, Godspeed,* and *Discovery*— dropped anchor in a waterway they named the James River. More than one hundred men and boys established the fortified village of Jamestown. In the first years, more than half the colonists died of disease and starvation.

The Jamestown colony survived largely because Captain John Smith took charge. He insisted that every man work and persuaded the nearby Powhatan tribes to help with planting crops. Chief Powhatan had mixed feelings about the settlers. He knew the Europeans could be dangerous, but he also recognized the value of trading with them. For a while, the two groups worked together.

After injuries forced Smith to go back to England, the colony again experienced a "starving time." In spite of these difficulties, more settlers came with more supplies.

Then, around 1612, settler John Rolfe discovered that tobacco grew well in Virginia's climate and could be profitable. Virginians rushed to take more tobacco land from the

Native Americans. Powhatan grew angry when he realized the English had come "not for trade but to invade my people and possess my country." Tensions between the Native Americans and the settlers grew.

Plantations

The tobacco trade strained relations between the Native Americans and the colonists. In time, this trade led to suffering for another group—enslaved African Americans. Tobacco profits helped make the Virginia colony a success and plantation owners rich. At first, the planters hired indentured servants from England to work the fields. An indentured servant signed a contract, or indenture, to work for three to seven years, in return for their passage to the new world. Many workers hoped to start new lives in the new land after their years of service were over.

In 1619, English pirates brought the first Africans to Virginia, including Anthony and Isabella, whose child William was the first baby of African descent to be baptized in English North America. (In his account of the arrival, John Rolfe misleadingly wrote that the Africans were brought by Dutch sailors, a point that contemporary historians have disproven.) Many other ships carrying Africans who had been captured and forcibly removed from their homeland soon followed. At first, some of the Africans were considered indentured servants, like many white servants. By 1661, however, laws were passed declaring that the new arrivals from Africa were "bound for life." Slavery was made official, and indentured servants were no longer needed.

As the Virginia colony prospered, settlers pushed farther into Powhatan lands. In the early 1620s, the Native Americans fought back,

The Native People of Virginia

When the European settlers arrived in Virginia, there were some fifty thousand members of various tribes in the region. They are divided into three groups based on their language. Groups who spoke Algonquian languages lived on the coast. These include the Croatan tribe and tribes of the Powhatan Confederacy. The inland Cherokee and Tuscarora tribes spoke Iroquoian languages. The Catawba, Tutelo, and Saponi tribes spoke Sioux dialects. The Yuchi spoke a language that doesn't seem to be related to any other language.

The tribes shared many similarities. They got their food from a combination of hunting (for deer, turkeys, and small game) and agriculture (maize, squash, and beans), as well as some foraging for wild food. Earlier in their cultures, they hunted with spears and atlatls. By the time of European contact, they had transitioned to bows and arrows. All of the cultures made pottery, and they fashioned clothes and decorative items from leather and woven textiles. There was even trade between the tribes.

Tribes in the Powhatan Confederation ruled much of coastal Virginia. Their relations with English settlers varied between friendly and hostile. Later, many of the tribes signed treaties. As more colonists arrived demanding land, though, tensions rose. In the nineteenth century, the tribes were forced off their **reservations** and lost their official status as tribes. Some ended up in Oklahoma, such as the Cherokee and the Yuchi. Others joined with relatives from larger tribes. Among these were the Tuscarora, who went to New York and southern Ontario to join the northern tribes of the Iroquois Confederacy. Some of the Tuscarora live in North Carolina.

Today, the Commonwealth of Virginia recognizes eleven tribes, which are members of, or descendants of, the original groups present at the time of English colonization. They are the Cheroenhaka, Chickahominy, Eastern Chickahominy, Mattaponi, Monacan Nation,

Nansemond, Nottoway, Pamunkey, Patawomeck, Rappahannock, and Upper Mattaponi tribes. The Chickahominy, Eastern Chickahominy, Upper Mattaponi, Rappahannock, Monacan, and Nansemond tribes received federal recognition in 2018. The Pamunkey tribe received federal recognition two years earlier.

Spotlight on the Powhatan Confederation

Paramount Chief Powhatan: Eight of the eleven tribes recognized by Virginia are descendants of the Powhatan Confederation. In the late 1500s and early 1600s, many tribes were united under one strong leader named Wahunsenacawh, who is generally known as Chief Powhatan. Each of the thirty tribes he ruled had their own chief, known as a *weroance* (male chief) or *weroansqua* (female chief), but Powhatan was considered the **paramount** chief, ruling them all.

Food: Duties were mostly divided by gender, with men hunting, and women growing crops of the "**three sisters**"—maize, squash, and beans—and also gathering wild bounty such as nuts. Both men and women probably fished and gathered shellfish.

Houses: The Powhatan peoples built shelters by bending tall, supple saplings into a framework for a domed longhouse. They then covered the frame with mats woven from reeds or grasses, or with bark. Some historians think only the high-ranking members of the tribe had bark coverings because bark was more scarce and harder to get than reeds.

Villages: The Powhatan tribes moved their entire villages periodically. Without the use of fertilizer or crop rotation, the agricultural land was eventually exhausted. After a while, game, too, became scarce. They would pack up their houses (reusing a lot of the materials) and move to a new, more fertile place.

John Smith's *General Historie of Virginia* included this hand-colored woodcut showing Chief Powhatan.

killing about 350 settlers. In 1624, King James I canceled the Virginia Company's charter and made Virginia America's first royal colony instead. He also appointed a governor. More settlers arrived, and by 1700, practically all traces of the Algonquian people were gone. Wars and disease had wiped out many of them. The surviving Native Americans had either given up their traditional ways of life to join white society or moved.

By the 1770s, Virginia was a thriving colony of about 120,000 people. Many families lived on small farms, but the wealthy plantation owners dominated the economy, social life, and government.

Independent Spirits

Through the 1600s and 1700s, Virginians had become accustomed to governing themselves. In 1619, they established their own legislature, or lawmaking body. This legislature, called the House of Burgesses, was one of the first steps toward self-government and democracy in North America.

In 1676, when the royal governor tried to establish tighter control, a colonist named Nathaniel Bacon led an uprising against him. The uprising, called Bacon's Rebellion, did not last long, but it revealed an independent colonial spirit almost one hundred years before the American Revolution.

By the 1750s, some bold pioneers had pushed beyond the mountains into the Ohio River valley, where they ran into fierce opposition from Native American tribes. The French, who had established a colony in present-day Canada, supported the tribes. The French were also interested in establishing forts and fur-trading outposts in the region. In 1754, George Washington, then

Christmas in colonial America was not as elaborate as today's holiday celebrations. On Christmas Day, it was important to feast on a good meal, and many early Virginians enjoyed dancing, cards, and other entertainment. A visitor to colonial Virginia wrote in 1773 that "guns were fired all round the House" on Christmas morning, waking him up.

Holiday Traditions in Colonial Williamsburg

Virginians loved to sing Christmas carols and hymns to celebrate. They decorated their homes and churches with green branches of holly, ivy, and mountain laurel. They also used fragrant herbs like rosemary, rose petals, and lavender. They attended church services as well. Gifts were simple, such as sweets or gloves.

Elaborate wreaths adorn Colonial Williamsburg during the Christmas season.

Today in Colonial Williamsburg, newer, more elaborate traditions have developed. For instance, since 1936, candles have been lit in certain windows in the historical area. In 1936, there were four candles, but as electric candles became available, more were added. This tradition has spread well beyond Williamsburg. Cressets are iron baskets hung on tall poles that hold flames to light up the night all through the town. Fireworks are the modern-day version of Christmas gunshots. Small street fires add to the Grand Illumination.

In Williamsburg today, the tradition of decorating with greenery has evolved into making very fancy wreaths with apples, pineapples, pinecones, and other decorations. Colonial Williamsburg's historical area during Christmas 2017 featured 2,552 wreaths!

a lieutenant colonel in the Virginia militia, led a group of militiamen to establish a fort in what is now western Pennsylvania.

Washington and his men were forced back by the French. That incident was the start of a long war in which Britain, with the help of the thirteen colonies and some Native American allies, fought against France and its Native American allies. Known as the French and Indian War (1754–1763), the conflict ended with a British victory. As a result, France lost to Great Britain virtually all the land it had colonized or claimed in North America east of the Mississippi River.

Taxes and Tea

Great Britain needed money to pay for the war—and to govern its huge empire—so King George III decided to **tax** the colonies. Many colonists were very angry. Any taxes in the past had always been voted on by each colony's legislature, such as Virginia's House of Burgesses. Since the colonists had no representatives in the British legislature, or Parliament, which was responsible for imposing the new taxes, their rallying cry became "No taxation without representation!"

The protests continued from the 1760s to 1775. Much of the action occurred in New England. The Boston Massacre, a skirmish in which British soldiers killed five colonists, took place in 1770. In the Boston Tea Party, colonists protested the British tax on tea by throwing chests of tea from British ships. Those who wanted to dissolve bonds with Britain were called patriots; those who wanted to stay united with Britain were called loyalists.

In September 1774, the First Continental Congress met in Philadelphia. It had delegates from twelve of the thirteen colonies, including

Virginia. At the time, delegates hoped to settle their problems with Great Britain peacefully. They were not intent on independence. Delegates from Virginia included George Washington, Patrick Henry, and Peyton Randolph. Randolph was elected president of the Congress.

In March 1775, the Virginia governor suspended the House of Burgesses. Many representatives continued to meet in a church. At one meeting, the patriot Patrick Henry delivered a passionate speech, urging the representatives to take up arms against Britain in self-defense. He ended with the ringing challenge, "I know not what course others may take; but as for me, give me liberty, or give me death!" One month later, fighting broke out at the Battles of Lexington and Concord in Massachusetts. When news came of these conflicts, Virginia patriots were ready to fight for independence.

Virginian Patrick Henry gave a stirring speech that encouraged colonists to stand up to Great Britain.

Declaring Independence

Soon after war broke out, the Second Continental Congress began meeting in Philadelphia in May 1775. Over the months that followed, the Congress made several important decisions. It named George Washington commander of the Continental Army. The delegates also discussed whether they should declare independence from Britain. In June 1776, Virginia delegate and lawyer Richard Henry Lee introduced a resolution asking the Congress to vote for independence.

Another Virginia delegate, Thomas Jefferson, was the main author of the Declaration of Independence. One of the celebrated documents of American democracy, the declaration stated, in clear and eloquent language, the principles that all people are entitled to freedom and equal treatment and that government should

The Declaration of Independence was written mainly by Virginian Thomas Jefferson.

serve the people. Based on these principles, the declaration went on to give the reasons why the thirteen colonies deserved to be free and independent states. The Congress voted in favor of Lee's resolution on July 2, and it accepted the Declaration of Independence on July 4, 1776.

George Washington kept his poorly equipped army together until, in 1781, with the help of the French, they trapped the main British army at Yorktown, Virginia. The battered British surrendered, though the war was not officially over until the signing of the Treaty of Paris in 1783.

Virginian James Madison is sometimes called the "Father of the Constitution."

We, the People

The Americans achieved a stable government when representatives met in Philadelphia in 1787 to write a **constitution** for the new nation. James Madison, a representative from Virginia, played a key role in creating the document that established the structure and powers of the US government. The US Constitution was officially approved, or ratified, in 1788. Many Americans, including Patrick Henry, had opposed the Constitution because they feared a national government that might become too powerful. Alexander Hamilton, John Jay, and Madison wrote brilliant essays defending the Constitution. Their essays were published as the Federalist Papers. That helped persuade enough states to ratify it, as did George Washington's willingness to serve as the nation's first president.

Divided Loyalties

In the years following independence, Americans wrestled with the basic question of slavery. How could Americans believe in the ideal that "all men are created equal," as Jefferson had written in the Declaration of Independence, yet still allow slavery? By the 1820s, most of the states in the North had **abolished** slavery. In the South, however, where the plantations needed cheap or free labor, slavery was considered a necessity.

Some Southerners, including plantation owners, felt that slavery was wrong, though that did not stop many from keeping their slaves. For some, the decision was purely economic—they could not afford to run their large-scale plantations without slave labor. George Washington was one planter who arranged to have his slaves freed after his death. Thomas Jefferson struggled with the question of slavery but claimed he could not find a way to manage Monticello without slaves.

Between 1820 and 1860, the North and the South drifted further apart. Many Virginians, and others in the South, felt that the North was beginning to dominate the nation's economy and government. It seemed to them that the North's power threatened not just slavery but their entire way of life. Some Southerners who did not support slavery, such as the Quakers, moved west as pioneers to form new free states.

One of America's largest slave uprisings took place in Virginia in August 1831. More than forty slaves, led by an enslaved man named Nat Turner, killed fifty-five white people. Many of the rebels, including Turner, were eventually caught and put to death. In the aftermath, white mobs murdered almost two hundred black people, most of whom had nothing to do with the rebellion. New laws were also passed to restrict the rights of freed blacks.

When Abraham Lincoln was elected president in 1860, many Southerners were convinced that the government would force the end of slavery. At first, seven Southern states—Alabama, Florida, Georgia, Louisiana, Mississippi, South Carolina, and Texas—decided to secede from, or leave, the Union (the

The Battle of Fredericksburg took place in December 1862.

United States). They formed an independent nation, the Confederate States of America, which is also known as the Confederacy.

The Civil War

The people of Virginia decided not to leave the Union unless war between the North and South was unavoidable. But Confederate forces attacked Fort Sumter in South Carolina in April 1861. President Lincoln then called for volunteers to join the army and fight to reunite the Union. Virginia, along with Arkansas, North Carolina, and Tennessee, then decided to join the Confederacy. Richmond was named the capital of the Confederate States of America soon after.

General Robert E. Lee was just one Virginian who struggled with the problem of divided loyalties. Lee was a member of Virginia's planter class and owned slaves, but he hoped slavery would end gradually. He also believed secession was unconstitutional. A member of the US military, Lee had graduated second in his class from the US Military Academy at West Point. He was a brave and well-respected soldier. By the time the Civil War broke out, Lee had fought in the Mexican-American War and had served as the superintendent of West Point. When Lee was offered command of the Union armies, he resigned from the army. He could not bring himself to fight against his native state. Lee joined the Confederate army and became its best-known general.

The people of Virginia's northwestern counties refused to accept the state's decision. They voted to break away and form the separate state of West Virginia. West Virginia entered the Union in 1863.

Many people believed the war would end quickly in victory for the Union. After all, the

North had a larger population than the South and housed three-quarters of the nation's factories and railroads. Many Southerners, however, believed they were fighting for their way of life and their homes. Many soldiers did not even own slaves. They felt they were fighting off invaders who had attacked their homes. The South also had a well-trained cavalry and a number of outstanding generals, many of them Virginians. In fact, the South relied heavily on Virginia because the state had about half the South's weapons, factories, and railroads.

The war lasted four long, bloody years, from 1861 to 1865. Virginia paid a heavy price for its leadership of the Confederacy. Because the Confederate capital was located in Richmond, many battles took place on Virginia soil. More than one hundred battles—one-third of all the fighting—occurred there. Thousands of the state's young men were killed and thousands more crippled. In all, the Civil War claimed more than 620,000 lives. When the war did end in a victory for the North, the states of the Confederacy were brought back into the Union. Slavery was finally abolished throughout the United States. Four million people were set free.

After the war ended, General Robert E. Lee worked to help reunite the United States. When some people suggested putting up a statue of him to commemorate the war, he opposed the idea because he thought it would prevent the wounds of war from healing.

Thomas Nast's drawing shows the journey from Southern slavery to emancipation, featuring a freed family in the center.

The Industrial Revolution

Much of Virginia's story from the late nineteenth century to the early twenty-first century involves the start of modern industries and the development of urban and suburban areas. At the end of the nineteenth century,

This May 1865 photograph shows Petersburg, Virginia, with its cotton mill on the right, a corn mill, and sawmills.

FAST FACT

It wasn't until 1877 that women in Virginia could own property. In 1917, women in Fairfax County were put in jail for demanding the right to vote. The Nineteenth Amendment to the US Constitution was passed in 1920, giving all American women the right to vote, but the Virginia legislature did not ratify (accept) the amendment until February 21, 1952.

Virginia had many farming communities and few large cities. Today's Virginia has a small percentage of farming families and many people living in cities or suburbs.

These great changes, shared by all the states, were the result of the **Industrial Revolution** of the nineteenth century. Machines now performed work that, in the past, had depended on human or animal power. In the early 1830s, for example, Virginian Cyrus McCormick invented a mechanical reaper for harvesting wheat. By 1900, McCormick's machines, pulled by tractors, enabled farmers to harvest enormous wheat fields in a single day. Machines allowed farmers to produce more crops with fewer workers.

Inventions like McCormick's created new industries and new ways of working and living. By the early 1900s, automobiles, electric lights, and telephones contributed to the amazing changes in American life.

Textile mills (factories where cloth was made), long an important part of Virginia's economy, remained important through the early 1900s. New machines helped mills become more productive, but they still required human operators. Unfortunately, the working conditions in these mills were often very bad. Children, men, and women worked long hours for low pay in dark, cramped rooms with little fresh air. In the early 1900s, laws were passed to protect workers and improve conditions in textile mills and other factories.

The Twentieth Century

From 1929 through the 1930s, the entire country suffered through the severe economic times known as the Great Depression. People across the country lost their jobs, their homes, and their belongings. At its height, almost thirteen million people—one-quarter of the nation's workforce—were unemployed.

The government, after Franklin D. Roosevelt was elected president in 1932, established programs to help those Americans who needed it most. One program was the Civilian Conservation Corps (CCC). This program employed men to work on natural conservation projects. Some of their constructions, such as stone walls and shelters, can still be found in national parks today—ninety years later.

President Franklin Delano Roosevelt visits workers at a Civilian Conservation Corps camp.

Shenandoah National Park

In the 1920s, outsiders who had hiked, camped, hunted, and fished in the Blue Ridge began urging the state and federal governments to turn the region into a park. In 1926, the US Congress authorized the creation of a national park, but only if the land was donated. Hundreds of Virginians went to work, urging people to buy 1 acre (0.4 hectares) of Blue Ridge land for six dollars and then donate it to the government. The state government also gained land for the park by buying farms from those who wanted to leave.

Construction on the park began in 1931 when Herbert Hoover, who had a fishing camp in the area, was president of the United States. When President Franklin D. Roosevelt took office in 1933, he also eagerly promoted the park.

President Roosevelt dedicated Shenandoah National Park on July 3, 1936. The park, now over 200,000 acres (80,937 ha), is a sanctuary for one hundred varieties of trees and more than one thousand flowering plants. In fact, park personnel say that the Shenandoah has more species of plants than all of Europe. There are over 500 miles (800 km) of trails for hiking and horseback riding and dozens of trout streams. The Shenandoah National Park

Big Meadows in Shenandoah National Park is home to hundreds of species of plants, insects, and other animals.

website lists more than 50 mammals species, about 50 reptile and amphibian species, over 190 bird species, and at least 35 fish species!

The War Boom

In addition to the government programs, the start of World War II in 1939 also eased some of the effects of the Great Depression. American factories were put to work, at first making weapons and equipment for countries in Europe that the United States was helping. When the United States joined the war after Japan bombed the US naval base at Pearl Harbor, Hawaii, in 1941, even more weapons and supplies were needed to support the troops. Virginia's farms and factories produced many wartime supplies. Americans found work in these now-busy factories. Women were encouraged to work in the factories because many men were fighting in the war. This helped to expand work opportunities and changed the roles expected for women.

A female machinist works at a manufacturing plant during World War II.

Creating Modern Infrastructure

Construction on the Pentagon in Arlington, Virginia, started on September 11, 1941. When it was finished, the Pentagon was the country's largest office building, and at its peak, it housed almost thirty-three thousand workers.

In 1956, President Dwight Eisenhower's Interstate Highway System began to be constructed. The interstate changed the way that people traveled, worked, and lived. People began to rely on cars as they traveled longer distances. The design of cities changed to work with cars instead of pedestrians.

Since World War II, growth and change have continued to characterize life in Virginia. Coastal cities such as Hampton, Newport News,

Toads and frogs have fewer safe places to live than they did in the past. You can help these amphibians by creating simple habitats for them in gardens, yards, and parks. All you need to do is create a shelter and a water source.

Build a House for Toads

Materials:

- An old flower pot or other similar container
- A plastic bucket or plastic container (such as a margarine container)
- A shovel or spade
- A hammer

Directions:

1. Dig a few inches down into the earth so the pot can rest snugly in place.
2. Ask an adult to use the hammer gently to create a semicircular hole in the side of the pot, close to the lip. This will be the entrance.
3. Position the pot upside down in the hole you dug.
4. Put some soil inside to make it cozy.
5. Nearby, dig a hole large enough to hold your plastic bucket or other container.
6. Position the container so its top edge lines up with the ground. Put water into it to create a little pond for your toad.
7. Place some bricks or rocks in your "pond" so that an animal may climb out if they fall in.

In May 1942, this subdivision near Arlington was completed.

In June 1960, the American Nazi Party protested people sitting-in at a lunch counter in Arlington.

and Virginia Beach have become major population centers. Cities on the western edge of the Piedmont, such as Charlottesville and Roanoke, have also grown. As the federal government has increased in size, more government offices have been located in northeastern Virginia, near Washington, DC, and more people who have jobs in or related to the government have chosen to live in that area.

The Civil Rights Movement

Since the 1950s, Virginia has seen an increase in the number of women and minorities rising to leadership positions that were once available only to white males. A greater variety of jobs are available than ever before, and education is available to people who want to prepare for them.

The civil rights movement of the 1950s, 1960s, and 1970s helped to end the more extreme forms of discrimination that African Americans suffered under. In 1960, one of Virginia's first sit-ins took place in Richmond when black students from Virginia Union University went into Woolworth's and waited to be served at the lunch counter. Rather than serve the students, the manager closed the lunch counter. A few days later, a group of students called "the Richmond Thirty-Four" were arrested after a sit-in at the city's Thalhimers department store. Their cases went all the way to the US Supreme Court, where their convictions were overturned. (This means that their sentences were found invalid.) Thanks to their efforts and the efforts of other protesters, the Civil Rights Act of 1964 and the Voting Rights Act of 1965 helped to bring greater equality for these students and all Americans.

Another group of people who have benefited from recent social changes is women, regardless of ethnic or racial background. The

Voting Rights Act of 1965 helped not only African Americans but also many additional women who had not been able to vote due to expensive poll taxes. In the 1960s and 1970s, the feminist movement worked to improve equality between women and men.

The Twenty-First Century

In the new millennium, Virginians have faced many challenges. Virginia has been the site of tragedies that shaped the history of the country—and the world.

On September 11, 2001, terrorists hijacked four airplanes. Two of those planes were intentionally crashed into the World Trade Center in New York. One plane was forced down by its passengers. Another plane struck the Pentagon in Alexandria, Virginia. More than one hundred people lost their lives at the Pentagon that day. In total, nearly three thousand Americans died in the attacks. Virginians, and Americans all over the country, donated blood, gave money to victims' funds, and volunteered. Virginians united to remember the people who died on September 11, and the government made new policies to make sure that an attack like that would never happen again.

Tragedy again hit Virginia on April 16, 2007. A lone gunman killed thirty-two students and faculty members at Virginia Tech. At the time, it was the deadliest mass shooting in American history. Virginians showed just how strong they are by rallying together in the face of such a terrible event.

Virginians don't just show their strength in the face of terror, though. Every day, Virginians work toward making their communities great. In 2015, Virginia ranked sixteenth in the country for volunteerism.

FAST FACT

Virginia was the first slaveholding colony in North America, but in 1990, it became the first US state to elect an African American governor, Douglas Wilder. It was a long journey for the commonwealth to reach this point. For the first half of the twentieth century, black Virginians faced inequalities like not being allowed to marry whites or attend white schools.

Famous Virginians

Mary Julia Baldwin

At a time when girls did not have as many opportunities for education as men did, Mary Julia Baldwin studied at the Augusta Female Seminary, then taught women and African American children. When the seminary almost closed in 1863, Baldwin took leadership and transformed it into a four-year college. The school, now known as Mary Baldwin University, was renamed in her honor in 1895.

Ella Fitzgerald

One of the world's favorite jazz singers was Ella Fitzgerald from Newport News. Nicknamed "The First Lady of Song," Fitzgerald performed with all the great jazz players of the twentieth century.

Ella Fitzgerald

Thomas Jefferson

Arguably the most famous Virginian, Thomas Jefferson wrote much of the Declaration of Independence. He loved to learn and experiment with science and agriculture on his home plantation at Monticello. He played an important role in setting up the United States government and served as the nation's third president. He founded the University of Virginia.

Thomas Jefferson

Dolley Madison

Born into a Quaker family, Madison grew up in Hanover County. Her second marriage was to James Madison, one of the Founding Fathers and later the fourth president of the new nation. Dolley played an important role as political partner to her husband. During a White House fire in 1812, she rescued important documents and a portrait of George Washington.

George Mason

George Mason was the author of the Virginia Declaration of Rights, which served as a model for the Bill of Rights that gave Americans freedom of religion, speech, the press, and other rights. He refused to sign the Constitution partly because it did not have a bill of rights at first and because it did not ban the slave trade.

Pocahontas

Pocahontas was about eleven when English colonists arrived in Jamestown in 1607. John Smith believed that she saved his life during a misunderstanding with her father, Chief Powhatan. She married colonial leader John Rolfe and was renamed Rebecca as part of an effort to bring peace between her people and the English.

Maggie L. Walker

Born in Richmond in 1864, Maggie L. Walker worked for decades to provide opportunities for African Americans. Walker started a newspaper, founded a bank, and opened a department store. All these ventures helped African Americans to build better lives.

Booker T. Washington

Born a slave in southwest Virginia, Booker T. Washington walked to Hampton to attend Hampton Normal and Agricultural Institute. He worked as a janitor to pay for school. He helped integrate Native Americans into the educational program in 1878. Washington also founded Alabama's Tuskegee Institute. He believed education was the best path for African American progress.

Booker T. Washington

George Washington

Before he became the first president of the United States, George Washington worked as a planter (farmer), a surveyor, and a military general. He was born at Popes Creek near the Rappahannock River.

A woman hula hoops at a Manassas festival in 2011.

3 Who Lives in Virginia?

Virginians tend to be proud of their heritage, whether they are of African, English, German, Irish, Mexican, Chinese, Latinx, or other descent. Studying family history can be interesting, inspiring, and can give a person insight. Similarly, there are reasons to explore the commonwealth's "family history." People can remember the past to improve the future.

Some areas of Virginia, especially its urban areas, reflect the country's great mix of peoples and cultures from all parts of the world. In some geographic pockets of the state, however, there is very little diversity. Small communities on some of the Chesapeake Bay and offshore islands remained isolated from the 1600s to the late 1900s. The Chesapeake island of Tangier, for instance, is accessible only by boat or plane. The people there speak in a dialect unique to the area. For example, islanders pronounce "bank" as "bay-eenk." For "chair" and "scared," they say "churr" and "scurred."

The Earliest Virginians

Before Europeans came to the region, Native Americans were Virginia's only

FAST FACT

In 1924, Virginia passed a law banning interracial marriages. In 1958, Richard Loving married Mildred Jeter, but they were arrested because Richard was white and Mildred was of African American and Native American descent. The American Civil Liberties Union (ACLU) helped them fight for their marriage in court. On June 12, 1967, the United States Supreme Court ruled that states cannot ban interracial marriages.

human inhabitants. Today, however, Native Americans make up less than 1 percent of Virginia's population. The state has only two reservations—one is occupied by the Pamunkeys, and the other by the Mattaponis. Both groups are part of the Powhatan Confederacy.

Pamunkeys

The Pamunkey reservation is on the Pamunkey River. It includes about 1,200 acres (490 ha) of land. Thirty-four families live on the reservation. Other Pamunkeys live in nearby cities and towns. There used to be a Pamunkey school on the reservation, but now most Pamunkey children attend the public schools in King William County. The Pamunkeys have their own tribal government made up of a chief and seven council members. Elections are held every four years. The tribal government is responsible for upholding the laws that the Pamunkeys have established.

The reservation also includes the Pamunkey Indian Museum, which documents and celebrates the Pamunkeys' history in the state. The people are well known for their pottery, beadwork, and other art. They sell some of their impressive artwork to support the community, but most is created to honor Pamunkey traditions.

During the Upper Mattaponi Indian Tribe powwow, men from the group Falling Water sing, drum, and celebrate their heritage.

Mattaponi

The Mattaponi, "people of the river," trace their heritage directly to Powhatan, the great chief and father of Pocahontas. The Mattaponi reservation, one of the oldest in the country, was established in 1658. Located near the Mattaponi River, it covers about 150 acres (60 ha). About 450 people are officially part of the Mattaponi tribe, but only 75 of them live on the reservation. The Mattaponi also have

Make Your Own Apple Tansey

This recipe is adapted from *The Compleat Housewife* by Eliza Smith, which was published in London and in Virginia. Smith's book of recipes was the first cookbook to be published in the colonies.

Ingredients:

- 3 apples
- 3 tablespoons butter
- 4 eggs
- 2 tablespoons heavy whipping cream
- 2 teaspoons rosewater (optional)
- ½ teaspoon nutmeg
- 2 tablespoons sugar
- Lemon and powdered sugar to garnish

Directions:

1. Ask an adult to help you slice the apples thinly.
2. Melt the butter in a skillet and add the apple slices. Cook on medium heat until tender.
3. Meanwhile, take a medium-sized bowl and crack the eggs.
4. Beat with a hand mixer until they are foamy.
5. Add the cream and other ingredients and beat for 1–2 minutes.
6. Pour the egg mixture into the skillet over the apples.
7. Turn the heat to low and cook until the eggs are no longer runny.
8. When done, ask an adult to help turn the skillet upside-down onto a large plate.
9. Sprinkle lemon juice and powdered sugar over the top and serve.

Virginia's Celebrities

Gabby Douglas

Missy Elliott

Pharrell Williams

Arthur Ashe

Tennis superstar Arthur Ashe was born in Richmond in 1943. Ashe was the first African American to win Wimbledon, the US Open, and the Australian Open. Off the court, Ashe worked as an activist, speaking out about apartheid in South Africa and speaking up about HIV/AIDS.

Sandra Bullock

This Arlington native has appeared in such movies as *Miss Congeniality* and *Ocean's 8*. Bullock won an Oscar for her role in the 2009 movie *The Blind Side*. She is one of the world's highest-paid actresses.

Gabby Douglas

From Newport News, gymnast Gabby Douglas won a gold medal at the 2012 Olympic Games. She also won team competitions at the 2012 and 2016 Olympics. She is the first woman of color from any nation to become Individual All-Around Champion.

Missy Elliott

In 2004, Portsmouth native Missy Elliott won her third consecutive Grammy Award in the category for Best Female Rap Solo Performance. Elliott also works as a music producer and writes songs for other artists.

Jay Pharoah

Jared Antonio Farrow, born in Chesapeake, is a comedian, rapper, impressionist, and actor. He joined *Saturday Night Live* in 2010.

Pharrell Williams

Pharrell Williams was born in Virginia Beach. In seventh grade, he met Chad Hugo, and the two have performed together in The Neptunes and the band N*E*R*D. His song "Happy" was featured in *Despicable Me 2*.

their own government, including a chief, an assistant chief, and seven council members.

In 1646, the Mattaponi paid tribute to the Virginia governor. This old tradition continues today. Every year, on the fourth Wednesday of November, the tribe gives a gift of fish or game to the governor of the commonwealth.

Their reservation houses a fish hatchery, Baptist church, museum, community building, and marine science center. The American shad and other fish are important to the Mattaponi's diet and culture. At the marine science center, the Mattaponi monitor shad populations and water quality. They also develop educational resources that help communities protect their land and water. Pottery-making and other traditions are also still practiced.

A Mixing Bowl

The first European settlers in Virginia came from England. In the 1700s, colonists from other parts of the British Isles and Europe settled mostly in the Tidewater and the Piedmont regions. Farther west, hardy pioneers from Scotland and Ireland made their way south along the Appalachians and settled in the foothills of the Alleghenies and the Blue Ridge Mountains. Like some of the people living on Virginia's eastern islands, several hundred families became isolated in the mountain valleys. As a result, they developed their own crafts, making furniture, baskets, quilts, and musical instruments.

Throughout much of Virginia's history, people of African descent were largely isolated from the rest of the population. At the time of the Civil War, African Americans made up about 50 percent of the state's population. After 1865, that percentage steadily declined, as thousands of freed slaves headed north and

Emancipation Oak, where African Americans gathered to educate each other, still stands tall on the Hampton University campus.

west to look for jobs. The migration slowed in the late 1900s, however. Today, African Americans make up about 20 percent of the state's population, which is higher than the nation's average. The proportion of African Americans in the population varies within the state.

Many Virginians today say there are few signs of racial tension between white people and African Americans in spite of the state's history. Over time, Virginia has made many positive changes, including electing African Americans to local and statewide political offices.

Over the past thirty or forty years, Virginia's population has changed to include more people from different parts of the world than ever before. Immigrants come to Virginia from China, Japan, India, and other parts of Asia. There has also been an increase in Hispanic residents from Mexico, the Caribbean, and Central and South America. These groups have added a cultural richness to life in Virginia. As of 2017, about 62 percent of Virginians identified as "non-Hispanic whites," according to the US Census Bureau. The richness of diversity is expected to rise in the coming years.

Education in Virginia

Education is an important issue for many Virginians. The state has been one of the nation's leaders in higher education. For example, the College of William and Mary, founded in Williamsburg in 1693, is the country's second-oldest college. In 1819, the University of Virginia was established in Charlottesville, largely thanks to the work of Thomas Jefferson. The Virginia Military Institute, founded in 1839, is the nation's oldest state-supported military college. In 1868, the Hampton Normal and Agricultural Institute (now Hampton University)

In modern times, Virginia's population is changing dramatically. The most surprising and significant change, according to experts at the University of Virginia, is that the population is growing much older.

The Demographics Research Group studies the different parts of the population according to age, gender, race, income, and other traits. They found that the group of people age sixty-five and older is getting larger. At the same time, younger people are moving away. One reason this is happening is that during the 1950s, right after World War II, people had a lot of children—twice as many as during the 1930s. This was called the Baby Boom. These children are now retired adults. After the Baby Boom, people again had smaller families. Those children are now between their thirties and fifties. As more older adults move to Virginia and more young people in their twenties move away, the working-aged population is shrinking. In Charles City County, the sixty-five and up age group is expected to double by 2030. At the same time, the number of young families with children is likely to decrease. Since 2010, K–12 student enrollment has dropped in seventy out of Virginia's ninety-five counties.

More Virginians now live in cities than in the past, while rural areas have diminishing populations. Loudon County, Prince William County, and New Kent County are expected to grow the fastest by 2040. Buchanan County, Martinsville City, and Alleghany County are expected to shrink the most by 2040.

Virginia's racial diversity is expected to rise. By 2040, less than half of Virginians might be "non-Hispanic white," as the census describes. According to projections, the fastest-growing group will be Hispanics. Next, the Asian group will also grow. Meanwhile, the white population is likely to shrink more, and the black population is expected to remain fairly constant.

Changing Populations in the Commonwealth

Populations in Virginia's cities, like Alexandria, are growing more diverse.

Students in
northern Virginia

Virginia Military Institute

was created to prepare African American men and women to teach newly freed people.

Virginia's public schools for elementary and secondary schoolchildren, however, did not develop as early or as quickly. A law establishing public schools in Virginia was not passed until 1846—two hundred years after Massachusetts passed a similar law. Even then, the Virginia law was not strongly enforced. There were various reasons for this lack of interest in public education. Until the Civil War era, plantation owners hired tutors for their children or operated small schools for local white children. Local church congregations also established their own schools. Over time, however, Virginia did establish public school systems throughout the state.

In the 1960s, studies showed that Virginia's public schools ranked below the national average. Educators and parents worked to raise the schools' rankings. They formed committees to improve courses and pressed the state government for money for schools. The determination of educators, parents, students, and legislators has paid off. According to the National Center for Education Statistics, Virginia's fourth grade math and reading scores beat or equaled the national average every year from 1992 to 2017.

Strength in Diversity

Virginia's long history includes many vastly different groups of people. Sometimes those differences led to cooperation, and other times they have led to oppression, or unjust treatment. Virginians in the twenty-first century can remember the lessons of history. Some lessons are painful, but others inspire hope. The more that Virginians are able to work toward collaboration, the brighter the future will be.

1. Liberty University, Lynchburg

(45,754 undergraduate students)

2. Virginia Tech, Blacksburg

(27,193 undergraduate students)

3. George Mason University, Fairfax

(24,987 undergraduate students)

4. Virginia Commonwealth University, Richmond

(24,010 undergraduate students)

5. James Madison University, Harrisonburg

(19,974 undergraduate students)

6. Old Dominion University, Norfolk

(19,540 undergraduate students)

7. University of Virginia, Charlottesville

(16,655 undergraduate students)

8. ECPI University, Virginia Beach

(11,745 undergraduate students)

9. Radford University

(8,418 undergraduate students)

10. College of William and Mary, Williamsburg

(6,285 undergraduate students)

Virginia's Biggest Colleges and Universities

(Enrollment numbers are from *US News and World Report* 2019 college rankings.)

Virginia Tech

James Madison University

College of William and Mary

Large hay bales are a common sight on Virginia farms each autumn.

4 At Work in Virginia

Virginia has always been an agricultural state, growing tobacco for worldwide markets. Recently, the Virginia Economic Development Partnership identified additional key industries for the state. These are corporate services, food and beverage processing, information technology, life sciences, manufacturing, supply chain management, and unmanned systems (such as drones).

In 2018, according to the Virginia Department of Planning and Budget, some of the most abundant jobs were in professional services; local, state and federal government; trade, transportation and utilities; and education and health services. In 2017, Forbes ranked Virginia number five in the nation on their "Best for Business" list.

The mix of industries in Virginia reveals the same blending of old and new that exists in so much of the state's life. Some people work in traditional occupations such as farming and fishing. Others spend their time exploring Virginia's past by working at one of the many historic sites. Still others are engaged in manufacturing, research,

Around 10 percent of Virginians work in tech.

Cows graze in a Virginia field.

or providing services. Service workers include people in a wide range of jobs, such as government employees, teachers, health-care workers, and staff at hotels, restaurants, and shops, as well as all the tourist sites.

Farming, Old and New

For much of Virginia's history, most families lived by farming. Today, far fewer people are engaged in agriculture. Still, the state has more than forty-four thousand farms on 8.1 million acres (3.3 million ha) of farmland, which is 32 percent of Virginia's land. Around 90 percent of the farms are family owned.

Rockingham County in the Shenandoah Valley is one of the nation's largest turkey-raising centers. The state ranked sixth in the nation in 2016 for turkey production. However, chickens, or "broilers," are Virginia's most valuable agricultural product. Cattle also play an important role in Virginia's agricultural industry. Beef is the second-largest commodity in the state, and turkey is the third.

Soybeans and corn are also top crops. Soybeans are used in many products, including tofu, oil, soap, and crayons. The corn grown in Virginia is used mostly for grain to feed livestock. According to the Virginia Department of Agriculture, many of Virginia's agricultural products rank in the top ten among all US states. These include tobacco, apples, grapes, peanuts, and fresh tomatoes.

Food and Beverage Processing

Virginia's growing wine industry has made it one of the top grape-producing states. The commonwealth has almost three hundred wineries. Craft beer is another recently booming industry, as there are more than two hundred licensed breweries, compared to just forty-four in 2011.

Rappahannock News reported that Virginia's wineries attracted 2.25 million visitors in 2015. In 2015, there were 261 wineries, providing 8,218 jobs with rising wages. Virginia's wines are improving in both numbers and quality.

This vineyard is in the Blue Ridge Mountains.

Seafood

Since the earliest days of Jamestown, Virginians have relied on products from the Atlantic Ocean and Chesapeake Bay. Today, crab and oyster farms are scattered along the jagged shore of the bay. Shellfish, such as oysters, clams, and the famous blue crabs, are an important part of the commercial fishing industry. Flounder, bass (called rockfish in the Chesapeake region), and a number of other fish also thrive in Virginia waters. Offshore, many sea clams and scallops are harvested. Fishermen catch large ocean fish, such as swordfish and tuna, on baited hooks pulled close to the surface. These fishing lines can be 40 to 50 miles (65 to 80 km) long. Virginia is now the nation's third-largest seafood producer and the largest on the Atlantic coast.

One important type of fish is menhaden. The Algonquian Native Americans called it *munnawhatteaug*, which means "fertilizer." They used the menhaden to fertilize their crops—a technique they taught to the early settlers.

Today, people in small aircraft spot schools of menhaden and radio the locations to fishing boats. Fishers then catch the menhaden in large nets. As in colonial times, people do not eat the fish but use it for fertilizer. People also feed menhaden to their livestock, make fishing bait out of it, and use its oil to produce food, paint, and cosmetics.

The Newport News shipyard keeps busy with military and government contracts.

A New and Diversified Economy

The twentieth century saw major changes in Virginia's economic life. World War II, in particular, spurred the state's role in shipbuilding and in training bases for the military services. After the government hired the Newport News Shipbuilding and Dry Dock Company to build aircraft carriers and other warships for the US Navy, it became the country's largest shipbuilding company.

Since parts of Virginia are very close to Washington, DC, it is not surprising that the federal government is the employer of many Virginians. The headquarters for several government agencies are located in northern Virginia, including the Department of Defense (at the Pentagon), the US Patent and Trademark Office, the US Fish and Wildlife Service, the Central Intelligence Agency (CIA), and the National Science Foundation. Many Virginians commute to work in Washington, DC.

The Pentagon is located in northern Virginia.

Visiting the Past in Special Places

Visitors to Virginia can enjoy historical experiences at a number of magnificent plantations and the homes of famous Americans, including George Washington's Mount Vernon and Thomas Jefferson's Monticello. Jefferson's talent as an architect is also on display in the buildings of the University of Virginia in Charlottesville and the Virginia State Capitol in Richmond.

In fact, no state in the nation has more historic sites than Virginia, including early homes, plantations, and battlefields dating from the American Revolution and the Civil War. Restoring and preserving these sites, along with providing guided tours and other services to visitors, adds to Virginia's tourism industry, which supports 232,000 jobs. In 2017, tourism generated

a record $25 billion in spending. Some of the money people spend while visiting Virginia's sites, staying at hotels, eating at restaurants, and shopping in stores goes to the state government in the form of taxes. The award-winning slogan "Virginia is for Lovers," created in 1969, is still used to promote tourism.

Thomas Jefferson designed his home at Monticello. Today, it's a popular place to visit and learn about American history.

In 1926, a Virginian Episcopal priest named Dr. W. A. R. Goodwin shared with American philanthropist John D. Rockefeller Jr. his dream of preserving Williamsburg's historic buildings. Rockefeller agreed that an important part of the nation's early history might soon be lost forever. He gave money to help restore and develop Colonial Williamsburg, which today encompasses about 85 percent of Virginia's original capital city. The site includes eighty-eight restored eighteenth-century structures, as well as scores of reconstructed homes, shops, taverns, and government buildings.

More than twenty battlefield sites from the Civil War add to Virginia's tourism industry. The most popular sites for visitors include Manassas—known to Northerners as Bull Run—where the Confederates won two victories, and the village of Appomattox Court House. It was there, at McLean House, that General Lee surrendered

The Virginia Museum of the Civil War is located in New Market.

to Union general Ulysses S. Grant. Many other sites are located between Washington, DC, and Richmond, and in the Shenandoah Valley.

Virginia Is for Nature Lovers

Tourists also visit the state to enjoy its natural wonders. Many families enjoy camping in the state and national parks. The rivers, lakes, and streams offer great boating, swimming, and fishing. Many people go to Chesapeake Bay to enjoy the abundant water activities.

Virginia Beach is another popular tourist destination. It is said that this resort city has the longest pleasure beach in the world. Virginia Beach includes 35 miles (56 km) of waterfront property, a 3-mile (5 km) boardwalk, and plenty of entertainment, from restaurants and shops to live music. Birding trails, whale-watching expeditions, golf courses, and fishing competitions are other fun recreational offerings.

Virginia Beach is a popular vacation spot thanks to its sandy beaches and boardwalk hotels.

There are many new and emerging industries in the Old Dominion State. For example, Virginia is at the forefront of developing unmanned aircraft (drones). In 2018, the commonwealth won a bid to work with the Department of Transportation's project promoting the safe use and development of drones. The three-year project will test out drones for delivering packages, managing emergencies and traffic, checking infrastructure, and other uses.

New and Emerging Industries

Technology has also become an important part of agriculture. "Precision agriculture" means using new technology to make farming more accurate and productive. It includes using GPS guidance, robotics, drones, soil sampling, and many other tools to make farming easier. Researchers at Virginia Tech use cutting-edge technology, and students get hands-on experience through the school's College of Agriculture and Life Sciences.

This demonstration of precision farming in Bruington included launching a drone.

Overall, technology jobs have become an essential part of Virginia's economy. According to the Computing Technology Industry Assocation (CompTIA), an organization that ranks states according to their digital economies, Virginia ranks sixth in the nation for tech employment. It ranked seventh among all states in the 2017 Innovation Score, which is based on an analysis of new tech patents, tech startups, and new tech business establishments. The tech industry provides $57 billion to Virginia's economy, which is about 10 percent of the state's total economy. About 10 percent of the state's workers are employed in technology. These include software and web developers, cybersecurity experts, computer support specialists, and more.

ChapStick: A Virginia Invention

ChapStick was first invented in the late 1890s in Lynchburg by Dr. Charles Browne Fleet, a trained pharmacist. The first ChapStick tubes looked like a candle wrapped in tinfoil. Fleet could not find a way to make much money from the product. In 1912, he sold the recipe for five dollars to another Lynchburg resident, his friend John Morton, who worked together with his wife to produce pink ChapStick in their home kitchen. Mrs. Morton thought of using brass tubes to shape the product, then after it cooled, they cut it into sticks and put it in metal casings. The new packaging made sales successful, and the business moved from their home to a factory. This was the start of Morton Manufacturing Corporation.

In 1936, another Lynchburg resident, Frank B. Wright, designed a logo for the lip balm. It is the same logo that is still used today all over the world. In 1963, the Mortons sold the rights to ChapStick to A. H. Robins, a Richmond company. Starting in 1971, new flavors were added. The formula remains the same, but the tube material has changed from metal to plastic. Since 2009, ChapStick has been owned by the Pfizer corporation.

Women work on an assembly line in Lynchburg's ChapStick factory, circa 1962.

A Bright Future
for Virginia

Virginia has shifted from a tobacco-based economy (which dates back to the 1600s) to a much more diverse agricultural base, including wineries, breweries, and many crops. Newer industries such as aerospace and technology, government, health care, and other service professions provide a greater variety of jobs of the future. This diversity in the economy is good because even when one sector suffers, other industries can help to balance out the overall financial picture. As people age and live longer, medical research and health-care fields will grow in importance. People who enjoy computers and technology can find good-paying jobs. Meanwhile, education continues to be important in preparing people for all kinds of work. More than one-third of Virginians have college degrees, while others have pursued technical training needed to help them achieve their goals.

The Virginia State Capitol Building
in Richmond was designed by
architects Charles-Louis Clérisseau and
Thomas Jefferson!

5 Government

Virginia provided four out of the first five United States presidents, and three more since then. Early Virginians were very interested in the benefits of good governments and the harms of bad ones. They wrote many letters to each other about the positives and negatives of government. Today's Virginians continue to be invested in the role of government at all levels: federal, state, and local.

On June 29, 1776, Virginia became an independent commonwealth when its representatives adopted its first constitution. The constitution established an executive branch, two legislative houses, and a judicial department. The most important part of the constitution, however, was its Declaration of Rights.

Many of the ideas in Virginia's constitution later made their way into the US Constitution. This is not surprising because both documents were strongly influenced by the same man, Virginian George Mason. He wrote the Declaration of Rights. As a representative at the 1787 convention at which the US Constitution was written, Mason worried about giving too much power to the federal government. He successfully argued to add a Bill of Rights.

FAST FACT
Tim Kaine, former governor of Virginia, ran alongside Hillary Clinton as her pick for vice president in the 2016 presidential election. Although they were not elected, Kaine continues to represent the state of Virginia in the United States Senate.

This letter from James Madison to Thomas Jefferson is dated November 10, 1821.

George Mason is sometimes called the "Father of the Bill of Rights."

The first ten amendments to the US Constitution, called the Bill of Rights, guarantee Americans important freedoms, including the freedoms of speech and religion. They also give Americans protection from unfair treatment by the government. Mason's efforts earned him the nickname Father of the Bill of Rights.

Throughout the state's history, Virginians have been willing to make changes to their government when needed. The 1776 state constitution has gone through five major revisions. Other changes have been achieved by a simple act of the general assembly (the state legislature). In colonial times, for example, the Episcopal Church was the state's official church, but many people felt this was not fair to those who followed other religions or no religion. Thomas Jefferson devised a new law, the Virginia Statute for Religious Freedom, that guaranteed freedom of worship for all. Jefferson's law has been a model for other state constitutions.

A more recent example of how Virginia alters its government to accommodate changing times relates to the state supreme court. The general assembly appointed a commission to look for ways to help the Supreme Court of Virginia, which was being overwhelmed by too many cases. The state legislators suggested adding another court to hear appeals (requests for a court decision to be reviewed). This court of appeals would decide some of the cases. The supreme court would get the cases that involved a more complicated interpretation of the state constitution. The new court, called the court of appeals, went into effect in 1985. It has helped relieve the pressure on the state's highest court.

The court of appeals in Richmond

Virginia's Unique City and County Structures

Most Virginians believe that the structure of their government should be as simple as possible to respond to the needs of the people. To bring government close to the people, the voters in each of the ninety-five counties elect a board of supervisors to handle most local matters. Each town sends a supervisor to the county board. There are thirty-eight cities, which are usually governed by a mayor and city council. In Virginia, cities are independent from counties. Independent cities have their own governments and levy their own taxes. Cities can vote to become towns, thereby dissolving their own governments and becoming a part of the county. Bedford was the last city to do that, becoming a town on July 1, 2013.

All levels of the Virginia government work to help businesses. The Department of Economic Development, for example, which operates out of the governor's office, works with business groups to attract new opportunities to the state.

The state government serves a similar function for the arts. This involvement began during the Great Depression. To help the many artists who were out of work, the general assembly created the Virginia Museum of Fine Arts—the country's first state-supported museum of the arts. The museum, which

Senator Mark Warner (*center*) visits downtown Winchester with local city managers to talk with citizens and business owners.

The Virginia Museum of Fine Arts, located in Richmond, offers free admission to visitors.

opened in 1936, provided a place for artists to display their work. It also established a performing arts program, providing funds to support performances by local theater groups, symphony orchestras, and dance companies.

In addition to state and local government, Virginia is represented in the US Congress in Washington, DC. Like all other states, Virginia has two US senators who serve six-year terms. As of 2019, the state had eleven representatives in the US House of Representatives. Representatives serve two-year terms. A state's population determines its number of representatives.

The Commonwealth's Three Branches of Government

Executive

The governor, lieutenant governor, and state attorney general are elected for four-year terms. The governor's major job is to see that the laws are carried out. He or she appoints the directors of executive departments, such as education and transportation, who oversee the day-to-day work of the government. The governor can also propose new laws and can

The Virginia General Assembly at a meeting in the House Chambers on January 15, 2018

reject laws passed by the general assembly. Virginia is the only state in which the governor cannot serve two consecutive terms.

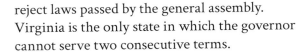

Legislative

The lawmaking body is the general assembly, made up of two houses—a forty-member senate, elected for four-year terms, and a house of delegates, with one hundred members elected for two-year terms.

Judicial

There are four levels of courts. The Supreme Court of Virginia, with its seven judges, is the highest state court. The state supreme court hears appeals of decisions made by the lower courts. Below the supreme court is the court of appeals. Below that are the thirty-one judicial circuits that deal with general court matters, trying both criminal cases and civil cases, in which someone seeks damages from a company or an individual. The fourth—and lowest—level is made up of general district courts and special courts, such as juvenile courts or family courts.

The 1917 courthouse in Chesterfield is still in use.

From Bill to Law

As in other states, before a law is passed in Virginia, it goes through an established process. Most laws begin with a suggestion or an idea from a Virginia resident or a member of the state legislature. The proposed law is called a **bill**.

When a legislator in one of the two legislative houses introduces a bill, it is assigned to a committee, which may revise or reject the bill. If the committee is satisfied with the bill, it presents it to the entire house. The bill is read to the house three times. After the second reading, legislators can amend—or revise—the bill. They usually debate the bill after the third reading. Then the legislators vote on the bill. If it is approved, it is sent to the other house, where it goes through a similar process.

If both houses agree on the bill, it is sent to the governor. If the governor approves the bill, he or she can sign it into law. The governor can also make changes to the bill and send it back to the general assembly. If the governor does not take any action, the bill will automatically become law after a certain amount of time. The governor can also veto—or reject—the bill. The vetoed bill can still become law if two-thirds of the members of both houses vote to override the governor's veto.

Testing the Limits of Power

The extent of the ability of the governor to use his veto power was tested in June 2014. Governor Terry McAuliffe wanted to veto individual items in the state budget. One of his goals was to expand health coverage under the Affordable Care Act. To do that, he wanted to veto an amendment to the state budget that said that Medicaid—which is how health insurance would be extended to the poor—could not be expanded unless the legislature allocated money just for that purpose. Virginia House Speaker William J. Howell found a rule that prevented the governor from doing what he wanted, and the legislature then passed a two-year budget.

Some members of the legislature argued that what the governor had tried to do was not allowed under the state constitution. The Virginia constitution requires the legislature to approve any spending, even if the money is coming from the federal government to pay for most of the Medicaid expansion. Other legislators wanted the issue debated, and the governor promised to explore other ways to expand health coverage.

A person is never too young or too old to pay attention to what the government is doing. Since the rise of the internet, it is easier than ever before for citizens to look up information about elected representatives, current and proposed laws, and ways to become involved.

The commonwealth has created a website where citizens can look up many important facts and pieces of information. You can find it at: https://www.Virginia.gov/government.

From this page, there are links to the Constitution of Virginia and the Virginia Government Organizational Chart, which explains how the government is set up.

From the web page, there is also the link for "Who's My Legislator" to find an interactive map to help you see who your representatives are.

Once you have identified your representatives, you can follow them on social media accounts if you have them. Always check with a responsible adult before setting up an online account. You can follow your officials on Facebook to see their updates and track important topics. Without a social media account, you can visit the websites for each elected official. There you can find contact forms if you wish to submit a comment or opinion. For example, some young people have helped to choose new state symbols by contacting their representatives.

Know Your Government

Virginia.gov is a great resource for Virginia's citizens.

In 2017, the people of Virginia elected a new governor, Ralph Northam, a pediatrician who promised to expand access to health care and to work productively with both political parties. Virginia has one of the lowest rates in the nation of Medicaid participation. In 2018, the Virginia General Assembly voted to approve Medicaid expansion to four hundred thousand poor residents, to take place in 2019. The process took five years.

Power and Responsibility

From its earliest days as a colony, Virginia has been an important voice in American politics. Virginians work together to brainstorm ways to make the state and the nation better and better. In many ways, Virginians have succeeded. Virginia is a vibrant and diverse place to live!

Glossary

abolish   To completely do away with, as in the abolition of slavery.

bill   A draft of a proposed law that has to be approved by a legislative body.

blaze   To mark a trail by making cuts in a tree.

constitution   A written system of principles and laws laid out for running a government.

estuary   A partially enclosed area where fresh river waters and salty ocean waters meet.

fertile   Able to produce a large amount of crops; supporting life.

indentured servant   A person who sells himself or herself into service for a fixed period, usually between three and seven years, often in exchange for transportation to a new land.

Industrial Revolution   A rapid change in the economy started by the introduction of power-driven machinery, which changed manufacturing.

paramount   Of the highest rank; the most important.

plantation   A large estate or farm, which can often operate almost like a village, with live-in laborers.

reservation   An area of land reserved for the use of Native American tribes.

stalactite   A cave formation hanging from the cave roof caused by dripping mineral-rich water (unlike stalagmites, which grow from the floor up).

tax   When a government collects money based on income, assets, or transactions. Taxes are used to support the government.

three sisters   A planting method using corn (maize), beans, and squash all planted close together.

Virginia State Map and Map Skills

Map Skills

1. What is the highest point in Virginia?

2. What is the northernmost city or town on this map?

3. What is the capital of Virginia?

4. What is Virginia's westernmost city or town?

5. To get from Emporia to Petersburg, what direction do you travel?

6. What bay is east of Virginia?

7. Which interstate runs north-south through Virginia?

8. What park is closest to Ewing?

9. What direction is Roanoke from Covington?

10. Which state highway connects Emporia and Virginia Beach?

Answers

1. Mount Rogers
2. Winchester
3. Richmond
4. Ewing
5. North
6. Chesapeake Bay
7. I-95
8. Cumberland Gap National Historic Park
9. South
10. Highway 58

More Information

Books

Hackett, Jennifer. *Virginia*. My United States. New York: Scholastic, 2018.

McClafferty, Carla Killough. *Buried Lives: The Enslaved People of George Washington's Mount Vernon*. New York: Holiday House, 2018.

Small, Cathleen. *Interracial Marriage: Loving v. Virginia*. Courting History. New York: Cavendish Square, 2018.

Websites

Capitol Classroom
https://capclass.virginiageneralassembly.gov
Explore links to information about civics programs, information about state emblems, games, and more.

The Official Commonwealth of Virginia Home Page
http://www.virginia.gov
Find official facts about the state of Virginia and browse the agencies that help run the state.

Virginia Museum of History and Culture
http://www.virginiahistory.org
Search the Virginia Historical Society's collections and learn about their exhibitions.

Index